Mountain climbing, speed skating, volleyball, waterskiing, and 23 other sporting activities are featured in this fun-filled book. Test your skills and see if you can spot all of the differences in the scenes while you learn a few interesting facts about each sport.

To do the spot-the-differences activities, first look carefully at each left-hand page. The page facing it on the right looks just the same—but it's not! Some things have changed, and it's up to you to spot all of the things that are different. As you find each one, draw a circle around it.

Try to finish the activities on your own. You can check your answers in the Solutions section, which begins on page 58. When you are done, have even more fun by coloring in the pages with crayons, markers, or colored pencils. Remember to look carefully!

Badminton is a racket sport that can be played
by two or four people.

Sports
Spot-the-Differences Activity Book

Tony J. Tallarico

DOVER PUBLICATIONS, INC.
Mineola, New York

Bibliographical Note

Sports Spot-the-Differences Activity Book is a new work, first
published by Dover Publications, Inc., in 2011.

International Standard Book Number
ISBN-13: 978-0-486-47527-1
ISBN-10: 0-486-47527-1

Manufactured in the United States by Courier Corporation
47527102
www.doverpublications.com

There are 12 things different between these two scenes.
Find and circle all of them.

Baseball is often called America's national pastime.

Look carefully and circle 12 things
that have changed in the picture.

7

Although professional basketball is played in an indoor court, the game is also popular as an outdoor activity.

This scene looks different.
Find and circle the 12 things that have changed.

Bowling is enjoyed by over 95 million people
in more than 90 countries.

There are 13 things different in the picture.
Find the changes and circle all of them.

Cross country skiing is one of the best aerobic activities
because it involves the use of the arms and legs.

Find and circle 12 things that are different
between these two scenes.

Diving is a sport that is part of the Olympic games.

There are 13 things different in this picture.
Find and circle all of them.

Figure skating involves spinning, jumping, and performing graceful moves on ice.

This picture is different from the other one.
Find and circle the 12 things that have changed.

Football is a team sport and has been played professionally in America since 1892.

This picture looks the same, but it's not.
Find and circle the 14 things that make it different.

Handball is played on a court where players hit
a small rubber ball against a wall.

Circle 13 things that are different between this scene.

Ice hockey is a fast-paced, exciting sport.

This picture has changed.
Circle the 13 things that make it different.

Jogging is a slower form of running.

Can you spot the 14 things that are different in this picture?
Circle them all.

Lacrosse is played using a solid rubber ball and
a long-handled stick with a net at the end.

Look carefully and you will find 14 things
that have changed. Circle all of them.

Miniature golf is also known as mini golf, goofy golf, and crazy golf.

What's different in this picture?
Find and circle the 14 things that have changed.

Mountain climbing requires great athletic and technical ability.

Find and circle the 12 things that are different in this scene.

Paddleball can be played by 2, 3, or 4 players.

There are 13 things different in this picture.
Find and circle all of them.

Ping pong, also known as table tennis, is a fun sport
that can be played by 2 or 4 players.

Can you find the 13 things that are different in this picture?
Circle them all.

Running is both a competition and a way to exercise.

Find and circle the 14 things that are different in this scene.

Although racing and cruising of sailboats are sports, many people enjoy sailing as a leisure activity.

This picture looks the same, but it isn't.
Find and circle the 13 things that make it different.

Show jumping is one of many English riding
equestrian events.

There are 12 things that are different in this picture.
Find and circle all of them.

When skateboarding, you should always wear
protective gear.

Look carefully at this picture and circle the 12 things
that make it different.

The sport of snowboarding was inspired by
surfing and skateboarding.

Find and circle 12 things that are different in this scene.

Soccer is the world's most popular sport!

Some parts of this scene have changed.
Spot and circle the 12 things that are different.

Speed skating has been part of the Olympics since 1924.

What's different in the picture?
Find and circle the 13 things that have changed.

Stickball is a street game similar to baseball.

Look carefully at this picture and circle
the 13 things that are different.

51

Tennis is a racket sport that began in the United Kingdom in the late 19th century.

This picture has changed.
Circle the 12 things that make it different.

Volleyball originated in the United States
over 100 years ago.

Find and circle the 14 things that are different in this scene.

An average of 17 million Americans water ski.

Can you spot the 13 things that are different in this picture?
Circle all of them.

Solutions

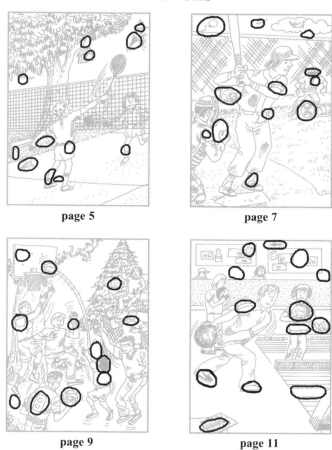

page 5

page 7

page 9

page 11

page 13

page 15

page 17

page 19

page 21

page 23

page 25

page 27

page 29

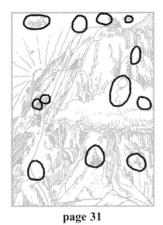

page 31

page 33

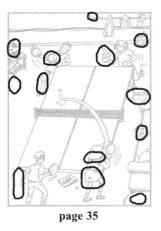

page 35

61

page 37

page 39

page 41

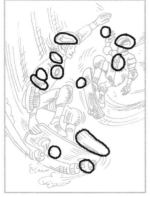

page 43

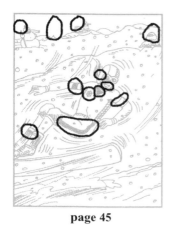

page 45

page 47

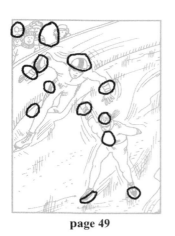

page 49

page 51

page 53

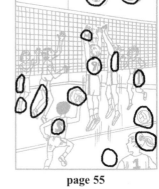

page 55

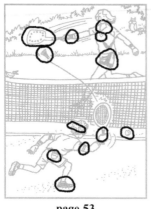

page 57